HOOKED BAGS

HOOKED BAGS

20 Easy Crochet Projects

MARGARET HUBERT

Creative Publishing
international

CHANHASSEN, MN

For my wonderful grandchildren, the sunshine of my life

Acknowledgments

I wish to thank Alchemy Yarns, Berroco Inc., DMC, Lion Brand, Paton, and Tahki/Stacy Charles Inc., who so graciously donated yarns for most of the projects in this book. Thanks to Jeannine Buehler and Paula Alexander for helping me crochet the bags.

Creative Publishing
international

President/CEO: Ken Fund

Vice President/Retail Sales: Kevin Haas

Executive Editor: Alison Brown Cerier

Senior Editor: Linda Neubauer

Photo Stylist: Joanne Wawra

Creative Director: Brad Springer

Photo Art Director: Tim Himsel

Photographers: Steve Galvin and Andrea Rugg

Production Manager: Laura Hokkanen

Cover and Book Design: Dania Davey

Printed in China

10 9 8 7 6 5 4 3 2

Library of Congress Cataloging-in-Publication Data

Hubert, Margaret.
    Hooked bags : 20 easy crochet projects / Margaret Hubert.
       p. cm.
    ISBN 1-58923-255-0 (soft cover)
    1. Crocheting--Patterns.   I. Title.
TT825.H798 2006
746.43'4041--dc22   2005031737

All the yarns used in this book can be found or ordered at your local yarn shop or craft store. Visit the following web sites for more information about the yarns shown:

Alchemy Yarns of Transformation
www.alchemyyarns.com

Berroco, Inc.
www.berroco.com

DMC
www.dmc-usa.com

Laines Du Nord
www.novayarn.com

Lily
www.sugarncream.com

Lion Brand Yarn Company
www.lionbrand.com

Patons Yarns
www.patonsyarns.com

Tahki/Stacy Charles, Inc.
www.tahkistacycharles.com

Contents

ABOUT THE PROJECTS 6

Kangaroo Pouch Shoulder Bag 8

Mix-and-Match Amulet Bags 12

Pocket Bag of Posies 18

Flower Embellishments 22

Shells Mini Bag 24

Summer Stripes Bag 28

Watermelon Slice Coin Purse 32

Bullion Stitch Backpack 34

Very V Hobo Bag 38

Tunisian Stripes Big Bag 42

Tunisian and Shells Wristlet 46

Festive Folded Square 50

Drawstring Petal Pouch 54

Bobbles and Beads Bag 58

Silk Victorian Pouch 62

Blooming Granny Squares 66

Shopper's Net Tote 70

Not Net Tote Tagalong 74

Eight-Pocket Carryall 76

Ninth Pocket 80

CROCHET STITCHES 82

ABBREVIATIONS 96

About the Projects

Bags and totes are very popular crochet projects. No wonder—they're fun, fast, and in fashion. Crocheted fabric can be tight (so the contents of a bag stay on the inside), delicate (for evening looks), open (for net bags), and shaped many ways. The opportunities to be creative are endless.

I designed my first bag because I couldn't find just the right one to go with a new outfit. I was short on time, but I crocheted a simple envelope-type bag, embellished it with a pin, added a shoulder strap, and had the perfect accessory. After that, I started making bags in all colors, shapes, and sizes, from the very easy to the much more complicated and free-form. My bag patterns were being published, and people were asking to buy them. I found myself making more and more bags, especially as gifts.

With this collection of my original patterns, you can make a bag wardrobe of your own. There are designs for bags in all sizes, in many shapes and styles, to be used every day or for special occasions. There are some "go with" projects: small bags that go into or attach onto larger bags to hold change, tokens, makeup, and other small things. These little bags can also become gifts for a little girl.

All the bags are easy, even if you are a beginner. Several bags are made using only single crochet, with interest added by colors and yarns. Others bags feature textural stitches that are easy to learn. If you need to learn or review a stitch, just go to the basics section on page 82, which has detailed, photographed instructions. For quick reference, pattern abbreviations are on page 96. For measuring, there is a ruler inside the back cover.

For each bag, I chose a yarn to complement the stitch and the style of the bag. Smooth cotton yarns show off the crochet stitches; they are good for decorative stitches like shell or popcorn, but they make even single crochet look fascinating. Cottons are also strong and durable, which is important for bags that will get a lot of use. Very textured novelty yarns are fun for bags, but the stitches won't show, so simple stitches are the way to go. For an example, see the Festive Folded Square, which is made with single crochet. The lovely silk yarn used in the Silk Victorian Pouch, and the ribbon yarn used in the Drawstring Petal Pouch, are not designed to take a lot of wear, so I reserve these special yarns for evening bags.

The materials lists will tell you the weight and type of each yarn, as well as the brands and colors I used to create the sample. You can substitute other yarns of the same weight. You can also use different yarns to create a one-of-a-kind bag. If you do not get the stated gauge, you may end up with a bag that is larger or smaller than the model, but luckily bags do not have to fit. There are so many yarn choices now. You can make something lightweight and airy, or fuzzy and woolly. Thick or thin, in any color—it's your choice.

The projects have a lot of special touches: handles, straps, closures, buttons, beads, and hooked flowers. You can switch these features from bag to bag. Put flowers all over the Very V Hobo Bag or the Bullion Stitch Backpack. Put a pocket on the outside of a plain bag. Change out the strap.

In the basics section are directions for lining a bag. While it is not necessary to line most of these bags, lining does enhance some styles. Most of the stitches are closely worked and create a fabric that is dense enough to keep small items from falling through, but some open-work stitches require a lining. I love lining bags in brocaded silks for a deluxe touch.

And love is what it's all about. I love watching my fabric grow, take shape, and become a thing of beauty. I hope you fall in love with crochet, too!

Margaret Hubert is also the author of Hooked Hats, Hooked Throws, Hooked Scarves, How to Free-Form Crochet, *and six other books. She designs crochet projects for yarn companies and magazines and teaches at yarn shops, retreats, and national gatherings.*

Kangaroo Pouch Shoulder Bag

You can take this stylish, slouchy bag everywhere.

The kangaroo pocket on the outside can be buttoned

closed. The bag is constructed quite simply from a

long rectangle folded in thirds; the outside pocket

forms almost magically. The bag is crocheted with one

strand of suede yarn and one strand of ribbon yarn

held together throughout, which

creates a dense fabric with

wonderful texture.

YARN

Medium weight ribbon yarn (A)

Shown: Suede by Berroco, 100% nylon, 1.75 oz (50 g)/120 yd (111 m): Clementine #3757, 3 balls

Medium weight ribbon yarn (B)

Shown: Zen by Berroco, 55% cotton/45% nylon, 1.75 oz (50 g)/110 yd (102 m): Gochu #8223, 4 balls

HOOK

10.5/K (6.5 mm)

STITCH USED

Single crochet

GAUGE

10 sc = 4" (10 cm)

NOTIONS

Stitch markers

½ yd (0.5 m) lining (optional)

½ yd (0.5 m) fleece or felt (optional)

Sewing needle and thread (optional)

Tapestry needle

Button

FINISHED SIZE

10" x 12" (25.5 x 30.5 cm)

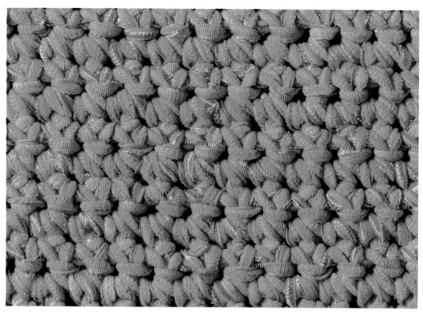

Two ribbon yarns worked together in single crochet.

BODY

Bag is worked with 1 strand of Yarn A and 1 strand of yarn B held tog throughout.

Foundation row: Ch 27. Starting in second ch from hook, work 1 sc in each ch to end (26 sc), ch 1, turn.

Row 1: Sk first st (ch 1 counts as first st now and throughout), sc in second st and in each st to end, 1 sc in top of tch (26 sc), ch 1, turn. Rep row 1 for 36" (91.5 cm), fasten off.

BOTTOM

Foundation rnd: Ch 20. Starting in second ch from hook, work 1 sc in each ch to last ch, pm, 3 sc in last ch, pm, working on other side of beg ch, sc in each st to end, pm, 3 sc in last st, pm here to mark beg of rnds.

Rnd 1: Sc in each st to marker, work 2 sc in each of next 3 sts, cont sc to next marker, work 2 sc in each of next 3 sts.

Rnd 2: Sc in each st to marker, [1 sc in next st, 2 sc in next st] 3 times, cont sc to next marker, rep bet [ ] once.

Rnd 3: Sc in each st to marker, [1 sc in each of next 2 sts, 2 sc in next st] 3 times, cont sc to next marker, rep bet [ ] once, fasten off.

Front pocket can be buttoned closed.

STRAP

Ch 5. Work as for body of bag for 38" (96.5 cm), fasten off.

FINISHING

1. Line the bag, if desired, following the directions on page 95. Line only 24" (61 cm) on the right end of the rectangle, as the 12" (30.5 cm) on the left end will form the outer pocket.

2. Fold the right end of the rectangle over 12" (30.5 cm) from the end. Stitch the vertical edge in place.

3. Join the yarn at the lower corner of free end. Work 1 row sc along vertical edge to 5 sts from top, ch 3, sk 3, sc in last 2 sts (forms buttonhole). Continue in sc along the upper edge of the entire bag.

4. Fold the free end over the bag, forming a pocket. Sew the pocket to the bag side halfway up to the top.

5. Pin the bottom section into place. Working from the right side through both thicknesses, work 1 row sc all around, fasten off.

6. Sew the ends of the strap to the sides of the bag. Sew on the button.

7. Cut 5 lengths of yarn B, each 10" (25.5 cm) long. Tie them around the button to form fringe.

Mix-and-Match Amulet Bags

This is a trio of neck bags known as amulet bags.

Decorative and beaded, these tiny bags are worn

like jewelry and often hold a charm or talisman.

Each bag has different stitches and decorations

that you can combine as you like.

YARN

Superfine cotton

Shown: Senso Microfiber Cotton by DMC, 60% cotton/40% acrylic, 1.52 oz (43 g)/150 yd (138 m): #1107 Nile, #1108 Light Pistachio, #1109 Light Peacock, 1 ball each

Each bag takes less than 1 ball of yarn; a small amount of a contrasting color is needed for the Picot-Trimmed Amulet Bag and the Popcorn Amulet Bag. To make the Side-to-Side Stripe Amulet Bag, alternate the 3 colors.

HOOK

3/D (3.25 mm)

STITCHES USED

Single crochet

Picot

Popcorn

Reverse single crochet

GAUGE

5.5 sc = 1" (2.5 cm)

NOTIONS

Tapestry needle

Beads for embellishment

Two strings of beads for strap

Three buttons for embellishment

FINISHED SIZE

3¹/₂" x 4" (9 x 10 cm)

13

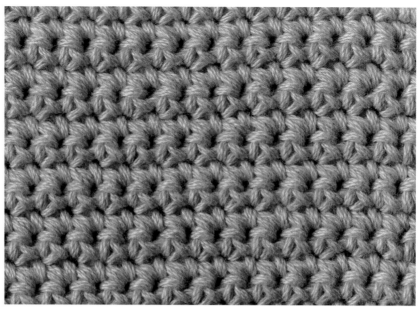
Superfine cotton yarn in single crochet.

Picot-Trimmed

Make two pieces alike.

Foundation row: Ch 21. Starting in second ch from hook, work 1 sc in each ch to end (20 sc), ch 1, turn.

Row 1: Sk first st (ch 1 counts as first st now and throughout), sc in second st and each st to end, 1 sc in top of tch (20 sc), ch 1, turn.

Rep row 1 twenty times more, fasten off.

FINISHING

1. Place the back and front wrong sides together. Join CC yarn at top right front. Working through both thicknesses, work sc down the side, across the bottom, and up the other side, but do not fasten off.
2. Ch 120 for strap and join to top right front (where you started).
3. Work picot edge as follows: * Ch 3, 1 sc in first ch of ch 3, sc next st, rep from * down side, along bottom, and up other side.
4. Work 1 sc in each ch of strap. When you reach starting point, join with Sl st, fasten off.
5. Sew three small strings of beads in corner.

Vertical rows of single crochet.

Side-to-Side Stripe

Make two pieces alike.

Foundation row: With MC, ch 21. Starting in second ch from hook, work 1 sc in each ch to end (20 sc), ch 1, turn.

Row 1: Sk first st, sc in second st and in each st to end, 1 sc in top of tch (20 sc), ch 1, turn.

Rep row 1 using the foll color sequence: 2 rows A, 2 rows B, 4 rows MC, 4 rows A, 4 rows B, 6 rows MC, fasten off.

FINISHING
1. Place back and front wrong sides together, forming vertical stripes. Join A yarn at the top right corner. Working through both thicknesses, work sc down the side, across the bottom, and up the other side, but do not fasten off.
2. Ch 120 for the strap and join to the top right front (where you started).
3. Turn and work sc back over ch to other side.
4. Work rev sc down the side, along the bottom, up the other side, end with Sl st, fasten off.
5. Sew three buttons to the front for embellishment.

Superfine cotton yarn in popcorn stitch.

Popcorn

Back: Ch 20. Work same as back of Picot-Trimmed (page 14).

Front foundation row: Ch 20. Starting in second ch from hook, work 1 sc in each ch to end (19 sc), ch 1, turn.

Row 1 (RS): Sk first st, * 1 sc in next st, rep from * across, 1 sc in top of tch (19 sc), ch 1, turn.

Row 2 (pc row, WS): * Work 1 sc in each of next 3 sts, [yo pick up lp, yo through 2 lps] 3 times in next st, yo and off all 4 lps on hook (pc made), rep from * 3 times, end 1 sc in each of last 2 sts, 1 sc in top of tch, ch 1, turn.

Rows 3–7: Rep row 1.

Row 8: Rep row 2.

Rows 9–13: Rep row 1.

Row 14: Rep row 2.

Rows 15–19: Rep row 1.

Row 20: Rep row 2.

Rows 21 and 22: Rep row 1, fasten off.

FINISHING

1. Place back and front wrong sides together. Join yarn at top right front.
Working through both thicknesses, work sc down the side, across the bottom,
and up the other side, but do not turn. Work 1 row rev sc over sts just
worked, fasten off.

2. String beads to desired length and sew to top edges for strap.

Pocket Bag of Posies

Crocheted flowers are so beautiful and fun to hook.

These pansies are blooming on a simple clutch.

The bag is a single-crochet rectangle folded like an

envelope. Add the strap, or not.

YARN

Lightweight cotton yarn

Shown: Cotton Classic by Tahki/Stacy Charles, 100% cotton, 1.75 oz (50 g)/108 yd (100 m): #3473 (MC), 2 skeins; #3476 (CC), 1 skein

HOOK

6/G (4 mm)

STITCHES USED

Single crochet

Half double crochet

Double crochet

Reverse single crochet

GAUGE

4 sc = 1" (2.5 cm)

NOTIONS

1/3 yd (0.32 m) lining (optional)

1/3 yd (0.32 m) fleece or felt (optional)

Sewing needle and thread (optional)

Tapestry needle

Button

FINISHED SIZE

10" x 8" (25.5 x 20.5 cm)

Lightweight cotton yarn in single crochet.

BAG

Foundation row: With MC, ch 41 loosely. Starting in second ch from hook, work 1 sc in each ch to end (40 sc), ch 1, turn.

Row 1: Sk first st (ch 1 counts as first st now and throughout), * 1 sc in next st, rep from * across, 1 sc in top of tch (40 sc), ch 1, turn.

Rep row 1 until piece measures 17" (43 cm), ch 1, turn.

Dec row: Sk first st, pick up lp in next st, pick up lp in next st, yo and draw through 3 lps on hook (dec made), cont in sc to last 3 sts, dec over next 2 sts, 1 sc in top of tch, ch 1, turn.

Rep the dec row 7 times more (24 sc), fasten off.

PANSIES

Make ten.

Foundation rnd: With MC ch 4, join with Sl st to form ring.

Rnd 1: Ch 1, [1 sc, ch 3] 5 times in ring, join with Sl st to beg ch 1. Pull CC through lp on hook, fasten off MC, cont with CC.

Rnd 2: [Sc, ch 1, 5 dc, ch 1, Sl st in next ch-3 sp] 2 times to make 2 large petals, [sc, 4 hdc, sc, Sl st in next ch-3 sp] 3 times to make 3 small petals.

Pansies crocheted in two shades of lightweight cotton yarn.

Rnd 3 (cont on large petals only): [Sl st in ch-1 sp, 2 dc in each dc, Sl st in ch-1 sp] 2 times, fasten off.

STRAP

Foundation row: Ch 4. Starting in second chain from hook, work 1 sc in each ch to end (3 sc), ch 1, turn.

Row 1: Sk first st, sc in each st to end, 1 sc in top of tch (3 sc), ch1, turn.

Repeat row 1 to desired length. Fasten off.

FINISHING

1. Line the bag, if desired, following the directions on page 95.
2. Fold the bag, wrong sides together, 6½" (16.3 cm) from the bottom. Mark the center of the rounded flap for the button loop.
3. Join yarn at the bottom right corner, work 1 row sc up the side, inserting the hook through 1 st of front and 1 st of back for each sc. Cont onto upper flap. To make buttonhole, ch 4, sk 2 sts, cont sc to bottom left corner. As you begin to join front and back on left side, make sure rows align across bag to right side.
4. At lower left corner, do not turn. Work 1 row rev sc over sc just worked, working 3 sts in button loop. Fasten off.
5. Hand-stitch pansies onto flap as desired.
6. Stitch the button onto the bag front.
7. Stitch the strap ends to the inside of the bag at the side seams.

Flower Embellishments

Hook a garden of flowers: a spider mum, a daisy (change the colors for a black-eyed Susan), and a thistle. Sew or pin a flower to a bag you crochet or even purchase, or to a hat or sweater.

DAISY

Use 4/E (3.5 mm) hook and cotton yarn.

Foundation rnd: With MC, ch 5, join with Sl st to form ring.

Rnd 1: Ch 1, make 10 sc in center of ring, join with Sl st to beg ch 1.

Petals: * Ch 10, Sl st in second ch from hook, sc in next ch, 1 hdc in each rem ch, Sl st in BL of next sc, rep from * 9 times more (10 petals in all). Fasten off.

Center: With CC, ch 3, join with Sl st to form ring, make 8 sc in center of ring, work 1 sc in each sc, fasten off, leaving a long end for sewing.

Thread long end on tapestry needle, gather around last row to form dome, and sew to center of flower.

SPIDER MUM

Use 6/G (4 mm) hook and 2 strands of fine yarn or 1 strand of light yarn.

Foundation rnd: Ch 5, join with Sl st to form ring.

Rnd 1: Ch 1, make 12 sc in center of ring, join with Sl st to beg ch 1.

Back row petals: * Ch 12, Sl st in second ch from hook, sc in next ch,
1 hdc in each rem ch, Sl st in BL of next sc, rep from * 11 times more, do not fasten off.

Front row petals: Working in FL of same sts in ring, Sl st in first st, * ch 10, Sl st in second ch from hook, 1 sc in next ch, 1 hdc in each rem ch, Sl st in next sc, rep from * 11 times more, fasten off.

THISTLE

Use 6/G (4 mm) hook and light cotton yarn

Foundation row: Ch 14.

Row 1: Make 8 dc in fourth ch from hook, turn.

Row 2: Working in back loops of the dc of previous row, *ch 6, Sl st in second ch from hook, sc in each rem ch, join with a Sl st in back loop of next dc, rep from * 7 times, do not fasten off.

Row 3: Working in front loops of the dc row, rep from * of row 2, fasten off.

YARN

Lightweight cotton yarn

Shown: Cotton Classic by Tahki/Stacy Charles, 100% cotton, 1.75 oz (50 g)/108 yd (100 m)

Lightweight silk yarn

Shown: Silk Purse by Alchemy 100% silk, 1.75 oz (50 g)/138 yd (127 m): 090m bronze

HOOKS

4/E (3.5 mm)

6/G (4 mm)

STITCHES USED

Single crochet

Half double crochet

Front post double crochet

GAUGE

Varies with yarn and hook

NOTION

Tapestry needle

FINISHED SIZE

2½" to 5" (6.5 to 12.7 cm) diameter

Shells Mini Bag

This sweet little bag can hold the essentials for a

summer event. It is also a perfect gift for a young

girl. The name refers to the decorative shell stitch.

Here is another way to make a handle: twisting yarn.

YARN
Lightweight cotton yarn

Shown: Grace by Paton, 100% cotton, 1.75 oz (50 g)/136 yd (125 m): Lilac #60321, 2 balls

HOOK
6/G (4 mm)

STITCHES USED
Double crochet

Front post double crochet

Back post double crochet

GAUGE
1 shell = 1" (2.5 cm)

NOTIONS
Square of washable felt in matching color for lining

Sewing needle and matching thread

Tapestry needle

Button

FINISHED SIZE
8" wide x 5 1/2" long (20.5 x 14 cm)

Front post and back post double crochet stitches form ridges between shells.

Yarn is used double strand throughout, except for sewing.

BACK

Foundation row: Ch 32. Make 2 dc, ch 1, 2 dc (CL) all in fifth ch from hook, * sk 2 ch, 1 dc in next ch, sk 2 ch, 2 dc, ch 1, 2 dc (CL) in next ch, rep from * across row, ending 1 dc in last st, ch 3, turn.

Row 1: * Make 2 dc, ch 1, 2 dc (CL) all in ch-1 sp in center of CL from row below, FPdc over bar of dc from row below, rep from * ending last rep with dc in top of tch, ch 3, turn.

Row 2: * Make 2 dc, ch 1, 2 dc (CL) all in ch-1 sp in center of CL from row below, BPdc over bar of dc from row below, rep from * ending last rep with dc in top of tch, ch 3, turn.

Rep rows 1 and 2, 3 times, rep row 1 once more (10 rows in all), fasten off.

FRONT

Work same as back.

FLAP

Join yarn (RS facing you) at beg of top right side of back, ch 3 and work same patt, beg with row 1, for 4 rows. On the fifth row, in center CL of row, ch 5 instead of 1 (for button lp), cont to end of row, fasten off. This reverses patt so that scalloped edge of shell is formed at end of flap.

STRAP

Cut 6 strands of yarn, each about 5 times longer than desired finished length of shoulder strap. Holding these strands together, fold in half and knot ends together. Pin knot to a padded, stationary surface. Holding yarns at fold, twist strands until they become tightly twisted and begin to crimp. Pinch strap at center and bring fold to knot. Holding twisted halves next to each other, release center and allow halves to twist together. Tie strap tightly, 4" (10 cm) from each end. To form tassels, trim ends and unwind to knots.

FINISHING

1. Cut two pieces of felt lining to the same size as the back and front of the bag, not including the flap (flap is not lined). Using a sewing needle and matching thread, stitch the lining to the wrong side of the bag back and front.
2. Pin the front and back, lining sides together. Using a tapestry needle and a single strand of cotton yarn, sew the bag together at the sides. Sew the bottom of the bag, joining at the top of the last row of shells. The bottom row of shell clusters forms the scalloped edging.
3. Sew the strap to the sides of the bag. Sew the button to the bag front.

Summer Stripes Bag

This bag is as refreshing and colorful as watermelon

on a summer day. Check out all the stylish

handles now available in yarn shops, fabric stores,

and craft centers.

YARN

Lightweight cotton yarn

Shown: Cotton Classic by Tahki/Stacy Charles, 100% cotton, 1.75 oz (50 g)/108 yd (100 m): #3764 (A), 1 skein and #3760 (B), 2 skeins

Medium weight cotton/rayon yarn

Shown: Cotton Twist by Berroco, 70% cotton/30% rayon, 1.75 oz (50 g)/85 yd (78 m): Sea Anemone #8336 (C), 1 skein

HOOK

6/G (4 mm)

STITCH USED

Single crochet

GAUGE

4.5 sc = 1" (2.5 cm)

NOTIONS

Button form

Pair of wooden handles, 5" (12.7 cm) wide

Tapestry needle

FINISHED SIZE

11" x 11" (28 x 28 cm)

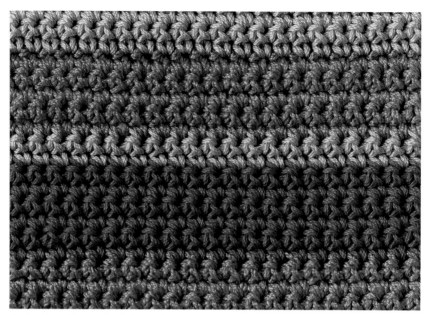

Lightweight cotton yarn in single crochet.

BACK

Foundation row: With A, ch 51. Starting in second ch from hook, work 1 sc in each ch to end (50 sc), ch 1, turn.

Row 1 (RS): Sk first st (ch 1 counts as first st now and throughout), sc in second st and in each st to end, 1 sc in top of tch (50 sc), ch 1, turn.

Rows 2–30: Rep row 1, using the foll color sequence: 3 rows A, 2 rows B, 12 rows C, 4 rows A, 2 rows B, 4 rows C, 2 rows B, do not fasten off.

Row 31: Cont in B, sk first st, pick up lp in each of next 2 sts, yo and draw through all 3 lps on hook (dec made), sc to last 3 sts, dec over next 2 sts, sc in top of tch (48 sc), ch 1, turn.

Row 32: Rep row 1.

Rows 33–42: Rep last 2 rows 10 times more (28 sc).

Rows 43, 44, and 45: Rep row 31 (22 sc).

Rows 46–51: Rep row 1, fasten off, leaving long end for sewing.

FRONT

Work same as back.

"Paper bag" bottom squares off the lower corners.

BUTTON TAB

Foundation row: With yarn B, ch 10. Starting in second chain from hook, work 1 sc in each ch to end (9 sc), ch 1, turn.

Row 1: Sk first st, sc in each st to end, 1 sc in top of tch (9 sc), ch1, turn.

Repeat row 1 for 3" (7.5 cm). Sk first st, sc in next two sts, ch 3, sk 3, sc in last 3 sts (forms buttonhole), ch1, turn. Sc in each st across. Fasten off.

BUTTON COVER

With yarn B, ch 3, join with Sl st to form ring. Make 8 sc in ring, make 2 sc in each st (16 sc). Mark beg of rnds, work 3 rnds sc in each st, fasten off, leaving a long thread for sewing. Place button form inside button cover, thread yarn on tapestry needle, and draw through each st, pulling tightly around button form.

FINISHING

1. Pin front to back, right sides together. Sew the side and bottom seams, beginning and ending at first decrease row.

2. To form the "paper bag" bottom fold, align the side seam to the bottom seam, spreading one bottom corner into a small triangle. Stitch from fold to fold at the top of the dark green section. Repeat on the opposite side. Turn the bag right side out.

3. Fold the top front over a handle to the inside, and stitch in place. Repeat for the back handle.

4. Hand-stitch button tab and button to bag.

Watermelon Slice
Coin Purse

The yarn left over from a bag project can quickly become

a little pouch to hold the little things that get lost in your

big bag. This whimsical coin purse was styled to clip to

the Summer Stripes Bag.

BACK

Foundation row: With C, ch 17. Starting in second ch from hook, work 1 sc in each ch to end (16 sc), ch 1, turn.

Rows 1–4: Mark row 1 as RS. Sk first st (ch 1 counts as first st now and throughout), sc in second st and in each st to end, 1 sc in top of tch (16 sc), ch 1, turn.

Row 5: Sk first st, pick up lp in each of next 2 sts, yo and draw through all 3 lps on hook (dec made), sc to last 3 sts, dec over next 2 sts, sc in top of tch (14 sc), ch 1, turn.

Rows 6–8: Rep row 1.

Rows 7–9: Rep row 5 (10 sc after row 9 completed), fasten off.

OUTER RIND

Row 1: Join B in right corner by marker, work 10 sc along row ends, 10 sc along bottom,10 sc along other side row ends (30 sc), ch 1, turn.

Row 2: Sk first st, sc in second st and in each st to end, fasten off B, ch 1 with A, turn.

Row 3: With A, rep row 2.

Row 4: Sk first st, 1 sc in each of next 9 sts, 2 sc in next st (inc made), 1 sc in each of next 8 sts, 2 sc in next st, 1 sc in rem 10 sts, ch 1, turn.

Row 5: Sc in each st, fasten off.

FRONT

Work same as back.

STRAP

With A, ch 38 loosely. Starting in third ch from hook, work 1 hdc in each st to end, fasten off, leaving a long end for sewing.

FINISHING

1. With black yarn, stitch four watermelon seeds on the front and back.
2. Holding the pieces wrong sides together, join A in a corner. Working through both thicknesses, work sc all around the sides and bottom. Sew the top closed on the green sections only, leaving the top pink open.
3. Fold the strap in half, sew it to one top corner of the purse.
4. Hand-stitch the zipper into the top opening.

YARN

Lightweight cotton yarn

Shown: Cotton Classic by Tahki/Stacy Charles, 100% cotton, 1.75 oz (50 g)/108 yd (100 m): #3764 (A), 1 skein and #3760 (B), 1 skein

Cotton Twist by Berroco, 70% cotton/30% rayon, 1.75 oz (50 g)/85 yd (78 m): Sea Anemone #8336 (C), 1 skein

HOOK

6/G (4 mm)

STITCHES USED

Single crochet

Half double crochet

GAUGE

4.5 sc = 1" (2.5 cm)

NOTIONS

Stitch markers

Sewing needle and black thread

Tapestry needle

4" (10 cm) zipper

FINISHED SIZE

3½" x 6" (9 x 15 cm)

Bullion Stitch Backpack

Bright colors really pop when they trim a deep color

like this purple. Most of this backpack is done in

single crochet, but the bumpy flap combines double

crochet with bullion stitch.

YARN

Medium weight cotton yarn

Shown: Cotton Classic II by Tahki/Stacy Charles, 100% mercerized cotton, 1.75 oz (50 g)/74 yd (68 m): #2924 (MC), 7 skeins; #2726 (CC), 2 skeins

HOOK

8/H (5 mm)

STITCHES USED

Single crochet

Double crochet

Bullion

Reverse single crochet

GAUGE

4 sc = 1" (2.5 cm)

NOTIONS

Stitch markers

Small amount of lining for flap (optional)

Small amount of fleece or felt (optional)

Sewing needle and thread (optional)

Tapestry needle

Cord stop

FINISHED SIZE

12" x 14" (30.5 x 35.5 cm)

Contrast row around bag bottom.

BODY

Bag is worked in rnds, starting at center bottom.

Foundation rnd: With MC, ch 4, join with Sl st to form ring. Work 8 sc in ring, pm for beg of rnds, bring up marker at end of each rnd, do not join after each rnd.

Rnd 1: Inc every st (16 sc).

Rnd 2: Inc every other st (24 sc).

Rnd 3: Inc every third st (32 sc).

Rnd 4: Inc every fourth st (40 sc).

Cont to inc 8 sts every rnd in this manner, always having 1 more st bet inc, until you have 96 sts.

Work 1 rnd only through BL, mark this rnd with CC thread.

Cont working in rnds on 96 sts until piece is 14" (35.5 cm) from beg, fasten off.

FLAP

Foundation row: With MC, ch 10 (RS). Starting in second ch from hook, work 1 sc in each ch to end (9 sc), ch 1, turn.

Row 1: Sk first st, 2 sc in second st (inc made), sc in each of next 5 sts, 2 sc in next st (inc made), 1 sc in top of tch (11 sc), ch 1, turn.

Row 2: Sk first st, 2 sc in second st, sc in each of next 7 sts, 2 sc in next st, 1 sc in top of tch (13 sc), ch 1, turn.

Rows 3–4: Same as row 1, having 2 sts more bet inc each row (17 sc). At end of row 4, ch 3 with CC, turn, do not fasten off MC.

Row 5 (bullion row): Sk first st, * 1 bullion in next 3 sts, 2 bullions in next st, rep from * across, end 1 dc in top of tch (20 bullion sts), ch 1, turn.

Row 6: (You will be working in the vertical bars behind bullion sts.) Sk first vertical bar, * 1 sc in each of next 2 bars, 2 sc in next bar, rep from * across, end 1 sc in top of tch, ch 1 with MC, turn, do not fasten off CC.

Row 7: Sk first st, 1 sc in each of next 2 sts, * 2 sc in next st, 1 sc in each of next 3 sts, rep from * across, end 1 sc in top of tch, ch 1, turn.

Row 8: Sk first st, 1 sc in each of next 3 sts, * 2 sc in next st, 1 sc in each of next 4 sts, rep from * end 2 sc, 1 sc in top of tch, ch 3 with CC, turn.

Row 9 (bullion row): Sk first st, bullion in each st across row, end 1 dc in top of tch (38 bullion sts), 1 dc each side), ch 1, turn.

Row 10: Sk first st, 1 sc in each vertical bar, 1 sc top of tch (40 sc), ch 1 with MC, turn.

Row 11: Sk first st, 1 sc in next 8 sts, 2 sc in next st, * 1 sc in next 9 sts, 2 sc in next st, rep from * across, do not turn, work 1 row rev sc, fasten off.

STRAPS

Make two with CC.

Foundation row: Ch 7. Starting in second ch from hook, work 1 sc in each ch to end (6 sc), ch 1, turn.

Row 1: Sk first st, sc in second st and in each st to end, 1 sc in top of tch (6 sc), ch 1, turn.

Rep row 1 for 35" (89 cm), fasten off.

DRAWSTRING

With double strand of MC, ch 100, fasten off.

FINISHING

1. With CC, work 1 row sc around the bottom of the bag in the free loops of the row that was previously marked.
2. Line the flap, if desired, following the directions on page 95.
3. Mark the center back of the bag and the center of the flap. Pin the flap to the back of bag, right sides together. Stitch in place.
4. Mark the center front of the bag. Starting 3/4" (2 cm) from the center mark, and 3/4" (2 cm) down from the top edge, using your crochet hook, pull the drawstring in and out at 2" (5 cm) intervals, all around the top of the bag. Pull the ends of the drawstring through the cord stop.
5. Sew the top of the straps in the center, behind the flap, adjoining each other. Sew the bottom of the straps to the row of CC at the back of the bag, having a 4" (10 cm) space between straps.

Very V Hobo Bag

Sling a hobo bag over your shoulder and you're

off. Hook it in a bright, happy color like this pink.

There are tiny Vs in the stitch pattern, and deep

Vs at the base of the handle.

YARN

Medium weight cotton yarn

Shown: Lion Cotton, 100% cotton, 5 oz (140 g)/236 yd (212 m): Fuchsia #146, 3 balls

HOOK

6/G (4 mm)

STITCHES USED

Single crochet

Half double crochet

GAUGE

17 sc = 4" (10 cm)

NOTIONS

Stitch markers

Tapestry needle

FINISHED SIZE

17" x 13" (43 x 33 cm)

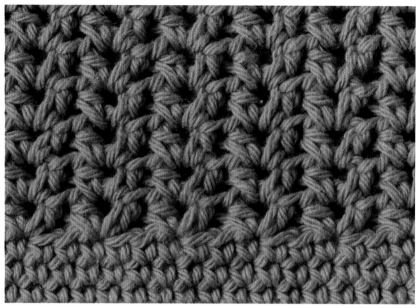

Medium weight cotton yarn in V stitch.

BODY

Bag is worked in rnds until top is divided for straps. Inc are made throughout by working 2 sc in 1 st. Dec are made by picking up lp in 2 sts, yo, drawing through all 3 lps tog. Make dec in the second and third sts from the beg, and in 2 sts before the last st.

Foundation rnd: Starting at bottom of bag, ch 4, join with Sl st to form ring. Work 8 sc in ring, pm for beg of rnds, bring up marker at end of each rnd.

Rnd 1: Inc every st (16 sc).

Rnd 2: Inc every other st (24 sc).

Rnd 3: Inc every thirrd st (32 sc).

Rnd 4: Inc every fourth st (40 sc).

Rnds 5–13: Cont to inc 8 sts every rnd in this manner, always having 1 more st bet inc until you have 112 sts.

Work even on 112 sts until piece measures 9" (23 cm) from beg, join with Sl st. Beg openwork V-st patt as foll:

Foundation row: Ch 3, * sk 2 sts, 1 hdc, ch 2, 1 hdc in next st (V st made), rep from * around, end 1 hdc in same st as beg ch 3, ch 2, join with Sl st to top of beg ch 3 (38 V sts).

Rnd 1: Ch 3, * 1 hdc, ch 2, 1 hdc in next ch-2 sp, rep from * around, end 1 hdc in last ch-2 sp, ch 2, join with Sl st to top of beg ch 3.

Rep rnd 1 for 6" (15 cm) more.

STRAPS

Working on only half of V sts, work 2 sc in each ch-2 sp of first 19 V sts (38 sc), ch 1, turn.

Working on these 38 sts only, work in sc, dec 1 st each side, every row, until 10 sts rem. Work even on 10 sts until strap is 17" (43 cm) from beg.

Join yarn other side and work second strap on rem 19 V sts to correspond, fasten off.

Sew straps tog at top.

Tunisian Stripes Big Bag

Tunisian stitch makes a dense, strong fabric, perfect

for a handbag. It is easy to learn following the steps

on page 90. You won't have to change colors

continually when creating these stripes, because the

pattern starts at one side rather than at the bottom.

YARN

Lightweight cotton yarn

Shown: Cotton Classic by Tahki/Stacy Charles, 100% cotton, 1.75 oz (50 g)/108 yd (100 m): #3815 (MC), 2 skeins; #3934 (A), 1 skein; #3722 (B), 1 skein; #3760 (C), 1 skein

HOOKS

10/J (6 mm) Tunisian hook

6/G (4 mm) crochet hook

STITCHES USED

Tunisian (basic)

Single crochet

GAUGE

5 sts = 1" (2.5 cm) on 10/J Tunisian hook

NOTIONS

Tunisian hook

Stitch markers

Button form

Piece of cardboard, 4" (10 cm)

1/2 yd (0.5 m) lining (optional)

1/2 yd (0.5 m) fleece or flannel (optional)

Sewing needle and thread (optional)

Tapestry needle

FINISHED SIZE

13" wide x 10 1/2" long x 2" deep (33 x 26.7 x 5 cm)

Lightweight cotton yarn in basic Tunisian stitch.

In basic Tunisian stitch, each row refers to both a forward and return pass. Forward pass is picking up all loops on hook; return pass is working them off. See page 90 for complete instructions for Tunisian st.

FRONT

Foundation row: With A and 10/J Tunisian hook, ch 53. Pick up lp in second ch from hook and retain on hook. Retaining all lps on hook, pick up lp in each st across ch, do not turn. Yo, draw through first lp on hook, * yo, draw through 2 lps on hook, rep from * to end of row, do not turn.

Row 1: Pick up lp under each vertical bar on prev row, retaining all lps on hook, yo, draw through first lp on hook, * yo, draw through 2 lps on hook, rep from * to end.

Rep row 1 using the foll color sequence: 12 rows A, 12 rows B, 12 rows MC, 12 rows C, fasten off.

BACK
Work same as front.

GUSSET AND SHOULDER STRAP
Using MC and 10/J Tunisian hook , ch 9, work basic Tunisian st for 60" (152.5 cm), fasten off.

BUTTON TAB

Using MC and 10/J Tunisian hook, ch 6, work basic Tunisian st for 8" (20.5 cm), do not fasten off. Change to 6/G crochet hook and work 1 row of sc along side of tab. When you reach end, ch 8 for button lp, then cont sc down other side of tab, cont along bottom, join with Sl st.

Work 1 row sc all around tab, making 1 sc in each st and 1 sc in each ch of button lp, join with Sl st to first st, fasten off.

Tasseled strap and crochet-covered button.

BUTTON COVER

With 6/G crochet hook and MC, ch 3, join with Sl st to form ring. Make 8 sc in ring, make 2 sc in each st (16 sc). Mark beg of rnds, work 3 rnds sc in each st, fasten off, leaving a long thread for sewing.

Place button form inside button cover, thread yarn on tapestry needle, and draw through each st, pulling tightly around button form.

TASSEL

Wind MC yarn 20 times around a 4" (10 cm) piece of cardboard. Thread yarn under loops at top and tie tightly. Slip the loops off cardboard. Tie another piece of yarn around the loops ½" (1.3 cm) below the top. Cut the loops at the other end.

FINISHING

1. Line the bag, if desired, following the directions on page 95.
2. Sew the short ends of the gusset together. Carefully pin the sides of the bag front to the gusset, placing the gusset seam at the bottom center. Using the 6/G crochet hook and starting at the upper left corner, sc in every st, inserting the hook through a stitch of the bag and the gusset with each sc. Work down the side, along bottom, and up the other side; fasten off.
3. Repeat step 2 for the bag back.
4. Beginning 2" (5 cm) from the top of the bag on each side, fold the shoulder strap in half, wrong sides together, and overcast the edges to form a double thickness strap.
5. Sew the tassel to the end of the button loop.
6. Sew the tab to the back of the bag, 2" (5 cm) from the top.
7. Sew the button onto the bag front.

Tunisian and Shells Wristlet

This bag is all about the stitch—Tunisian stitch and

shell stitch worked together using a lustrous yarn.

You do not need a special hook to work the Tunisian

stitch as there are only a few stitches on the hook at

any one time.

YARN

Medium weight cotton/rayon yarn

Shown: Cotton Twist by Berroco, 70% mercerized cotton/30% rayon viscose 1.75 oz (50 g)/85 yd (78 m): Sea Anemone #8336, 2 skeins

HOOK

6/G (4 mm)

STITCHES USED

Double crochet

Tunisian (basic)

Single crochet

GAUGE

2 shells = 3" (7.5 cm)

NOTIONS

Tapestry needle

1/2 yd (0.5 m) lining (optional)

1/2 yd (0.5 m) fleece or felt (optional)

Sewing needle and thread

10" (25.5 cm) zipper

FINISHED SIZE

5 1/2" x 10" (14 x 25.5 cm)

Diamonds of Tunisian stitch alternate with shells.

BACK
Foundation row: Ch 52.

Row 1 (shells): 4 dc in fourth ch from hook, * sk 3 ch, 1 sc in next ch, sk 3 ch, 9 dc in next ch, rep from * 4 times, end sk 3, 1 sc next ch, sk 3, 5 dc in last ch, ch 1, turn.

Row 2 (Tunisian st, RS): * [Draw up lp in next st and retain lp on hook] 5 times (6 lps on hook), draw up lp in next st and draw this lp through first lp on hook forming an upright st or bar, [yo and through 2 lps] 5 times *. There are 6 bars in row and 1 lp on hook. ** Lp on hook counts as first st so sk first bar, retaining lps on hook, and draw up lp in each of next 5 bars (6 lps on hook), draw up lp in next st and through first lp on hook, [yo and through 2 lps] 5 times, rep from ** 2 times. Insert hook in second bar, yo and through bar and lp on hook (1 st bound off), bind off 4 more sts, 1 sc in next st. Rep from * 5 times, end bind off 5 sts, sc in top of tch, ch 1, turn.

Row 3: Sk first st (ch 1 counts as first st), sc in second st and in each st to end, 1 sc in top of tch, ch 3, turn.

Row 4 (first part of shell row): Yo, draw up lp in second sc, yo and through 2 lps on hook, [yo and draw up lp in next st, yo and through 2 lps] 3 times, yo and through 5 lps on hook, ch 1 tightly for eye of half shell. * Ch 3, sc in next st, ch 3, [yo and draw up lp in next st, yo and through 2 lps] 9 times, yo and through 10 lps on hook, ch 1 tightly to form eye of full shell, rep from *

4 times, end ch 3, sc in next st, ch 3, [yo and draw up lp in next st, yo and through 2 lps] 4 times, yo and through 5 lps, ch 1 tightly to form eye of half shell, ch 3, turn.

Row 5 (second part of shell row): Work 4 dc in eye of first half shell, sk ch 3, 1 sc in first sc, sk ch 3, * 9 dc in eye of next shell, sk ch 3, 1 sc in next sc, sk ch 3, rep from * 4 times end sk ch 3, 5 dc in eye of last half shell, ch 1, turn.

Rep rows 2–5 once. Rep rows 2, 3, 4, fasten off.

FRONT
Work same as back.

SIDE GUSSETS
Make two.
Foundation row: Ch 6. Starting in second ch from hook, work 1 sc in each ch to end (5 sc), ch 1, turn.

Row 1: Sk first st, sc in second st and in each st to end, 1 sc in top of tch (5 sc), ch 1, turn.

Rows 2–20: Rep row 1.

Row 21: Sk first st, [pick up lp in next 2 sts, yo, pull through 3 lps on hook 2 times (2 dec) (3sts rem), ch 1, turn.

Rows 22 and 23: Sc in each st.

Row 24: Pick up lp in each st, yo, pull through all lps on hook, fasten off.

STRAP
Ch 6, work as first 20 rows of side gussets for 12" (30.5 cm), fasten off, leaving a long end for sewing.

FINISHING
1. Sew the bag front to the back along the bottom.
2. Line the bag, following the directions on page 95. Leave the top edges of the lining open, so the zipper can be placed under the lining.
3. Pin gussets in place, having narrow point at bottom of bag. Starting at top of gusset, working through both thicknesses, work sc all around gusset, along one top edge, around other gusset, and along other top edge. Fasten off.
4. Pin the zipper in place between the bag and lining. Stitch in place.
5. Fold the strap in half lengthwise, and sew the ends together forming a tube; leave 1" (2.5 cm) open at each end. Sew the open ends to the top of the gusset.

Festive Folded Square

This one's a breeze. A simple square folds up into

a fun bag. Stripes worked in single crochet alternate

between a textured, loopy yarn and a smooth yarn.

When you sew the bag up, the stripes run diagonally.

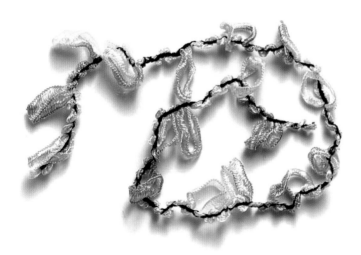

YARN

Lightweight cotton yarn

Shown: Cotton Classic by Tahki/Stacy Charles, 100% cotton, 1.75 oz (50 g)/108 yd (100 m): #3722 (A), 2 skeins

Bulky novelty yarn

Shown: Portofino by Laines Du Nord, 52% viscose/48% nylon, 1.75 oz (50 g)/74 yd (68 m): #57 (B), 2 balls

HOOK

8/H (5 mm)

STITCH USED

Single crochet

GAUGE

4 1/2 sc = 1" (2.5 cm)

NOTIONS

1/2 yd (0.5 m) lining (optional)

1/2 yd (0.5 m) fleece or felt (optional)

Sewing needle and thread (optional)

Tapestry needle

Pair wooden handles, 4" (10 cm) wide

Large covered snap

FINISHED SIZE

12" wide x 8" long (30.5 x 20.5 cm)

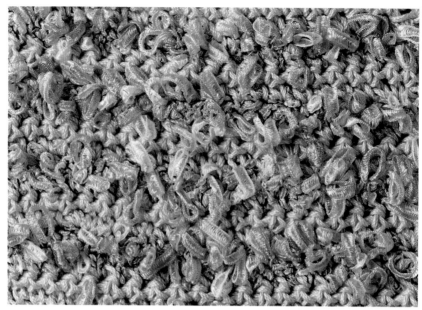

Alternating stripes of novelty yarn and cotton yarn.

BODY

Bag is worked in one square, using a striped pattern, and folded into shape. Yarn is carried loosely up the side of the work for each color change.

Foundation row: With A, ch 68. Starting in second ch from hook, work 1 sc in each ch to end (67 sc), ch 1, turn.

Row 1 (RS): Sk first st (ch 1 counts as first st now and throughout), * 1 sc in next st, rep from * across, 1 sc in top of tch (67 sc), ch 1, turn.

Row 2: Rep row 1, do not end A, ch 1 with B.

Row 3: Cont with B, rep row 1.

Row 4: Rep row 3, at end of row, ch 1 with A.

Rep rows 1–4, alternating colors A and B every 2 rows until piece is 15" (38 cm) long, ending last rep with A, do not break yarn.

Turn work at 90-degree angle and work 2 rows sc along side, fasten off A. Join A at beg of opposite side, work 2 rows sc, fasten off.

FINISHING

1. If lining is desired, cut a square of fleece 1" (2.5 cm) smaller in both directions than the crocheted square. Trim off two opposing corners 5" (12.7 cm) diagonally. Cut lining fabric ½" (1.3 cm) larger on all sides than the fleece. Center the fleece over the wrong side of the crocheted square. Place the lining over the fleece. Turn under the edge of the lining ½" (1.3 cm) and stitch in place.

2. Fold the two unlined points together and pin (these points will be turned down over the handles. Measure 6" (15 cm) on each side from the free points, and mark with pins. Fold the sides and pin the free points to each pin mark. Sew the sides, forming gussets. Remove the pins.

3. Remove the pins from the unlined points, and turn the flaps to the outside over the handles. Sew the handles in place.

4. Sew the snap halves to the inside of the bag, below the handles and just above the lining.

Diagonal seams transform the square into a handbag.

Drawstring Petal Pouch

This eye-catching evening bag was inspired

by a jester's hat. Four petal-shaped sections

made entirely of single crochet are sewn

together and drawn shut with a cord.

YARN

Medium weight ribbon yarn

Shown: Zen by Berroco, 55% cotton/45% nylon, 1.75 oz (50 g)/110 yd (102 m): Dharma #8228, 3 balls

HOOK

8/H (5 mm)

STITCHES USED

Single crochet

Reverse single crochet

GAUGE

4 sc = 1" (2.5 cm)

NOTIONS

Stitch markers

Tapestry needle

Bead embellishment (optional)

Sewing needle and thread

FINISHED SIZE

6½" diameter x 8" high (16.3 x 20.5 cm)

Ribbon yarn in single crochet.

PETAL PANEL
Make four.

Foundation row: Ch 2. Work 3 sc in second ch from hook, ch 1 (counts as a sc), turn.

Row 1: Work 1 sc in first st, 1 sc in next st, 2 sc in last st (5 sc), ch 1, turn.

Row 2: Sk first st, 2 sc in next st, sc in next st, 2 sc in next st, 1 sc in top of tch (7 sc), ch 1, turn.

Row 3: Sk first st, 2 sc in next st, sc in next 3 sts, 2 sc in next st, 1 sc in top of tch (9 sc), ch 1, turn.

Cont in this manner, inc 1 st in second sc and 1 st in next-to-last sc until you have 23 sc.

[Work even for next 7 rows, inc 2 sts in eighth row] 3 times (29 sc). Pm each side of piece at this point.

Beg dec as foll: Sk first st, pick up lp in each of next 2 sts, yo, pull through all 3 lps at once (dec made), work to last 3 sts, dec, work last st in top of tch, ch 1, turn. Dec 2 sts in each of next 5 rows, then dec 2 sts every other row until 3 sts rem, work 3 tog, fasten off.

DRAWSTRING

Using double strand of yarn, ch 80, fasten off.

STRAP

Ch 5. Sc in second ch from hook and in each ch across (4 sc), ch 1, turn. Cont to work in sc until strap is 20" (51 cm) long, fasten off. Fold strap in half, lengthwise, and sew edges to form rope.

Four petal sections sewn together; drawsting and strap in place.

FINISHING

1. Starting at the narrow end, pin each panel to the next, wrong sides together, inserting pins about 1/2" (1.3 cm) from the edge. Stop at the markers.

2. To join the pieces with sc and work all the edges with rev sc—working continuously—join the yarn at the bottom. Work sc through both layers up one seam to marker.

3. Working on right side of first petal (single layer), cont to petal point, work 3 sc in point, sc down to next marker, then cont through both layers to stitch next seam. Do not turn.

4. Work rev sc up the seam you just stitched back to marker. Cont with sc on next petal edge, 3 sc in point, sc down to next marker, then cont through both layers to stitch next seam.

5. Repeat step 4 for next seam and petal.

6. Work rev sc up the seam you just stitched back to marker. Cont with sc on next petal edge, 3 sc in point, sc down to next marker. All petal edges have now been stitched. Join with Sl st, do not turn.

7. Rev sc around all petal edges, back to the first seam. Rev sc the first seam, fasten off.

8. Weave the drawstring in and out of the stitches around the bag, 1/2" (1.3 cm) below tops of seams, beginning and ending at the center of one petal.

9. Sew the ends of the strap 1" (2.5 cm) below the drawstring, on the inside of the bag, on two opposing petals.

10. Stitch a bead embellishment to one petal point, if desired.

Bobbles and Beads Bag

Beads and crochet are wonderful together. This bag is embellished with a beaded trim, so you won't have to spend hours stringing individual beads (unless you like doing that!).

YARN

Medium weight cotton/rayon yarn

Shown: Cotton Twist by Berroco, 70% cotton/30% rayon viscose, 1.75 oz (50 g)/85 yd (78 m): Sensei #8345, 4 skeins

HOOK

6/G (4 mm)

STITCHES USED

Single crochet

Double crochet

Popcorn

GAUGE

16 sc = 4" (10 cm)

7 pc sts = 4" (10 cm)

NOTIONS

2 ft (0.63 m) bead trim on ribbon

Sewing needle and matching thread

Tapestry needle

24" x 24" (61 x 61 cm) lining (optional)

Button

FINISHED SIZE

8" x 10" (20.5 x 25.5 cm)

Bead trim caught in stitches between main bag and bobble strip.

BACK

Foundation row: Ch 43. Starting in second ch from hook, work 1 sc in each ch to end (42 sc), ch 1, turn.

Row 1: Sk first st (ch 1 counts as first st now and throughout), * 1 sc in next st, rep from * across, 1 sc in top of tch (42 sc) ch 1, turn.

Rep row 1 until piece is 7" (18 cm), fasten off.

FRONT

Work same as back.

POPCORN PANELS

Make two. These pieces are made separately, then sewn to the top of the back and front.

Foundation Row: Ch 36 very loosely. Starting in second ch from hook, work 1 sc in each ch to end (35 sc), ch 3, turn.

Row 1: Sk first st, * 5 dc in next st, take hook out of last lp, insert hook in first dc of 5 just made, pick up dropped lp and draw it through (pc made), ch 1, 1 dc in next st, rep from * 16 times, end 1 dc in last st, ch 1, turn.

Row 2: Work 2 sc in each dc (not in pc sts), end 1 sc in top of tch. Rep rows 1 and 2 once more, fasten off.

GUSSET
Ch 5, work as back until piece is 28" (71 cm) long, fasten off.

STRAPS
Make two.
Ch 5, work as back until piece is 15" (38 cm) long, fasten off.

BUTTON TABS
Mark center st on top of back pc strip, join yarn 2 sts before center st, work sc on 2 sts, 1 in center st, 2 more after center st, ch 1, turn. Sc on these 5 sts for 1 row, ch 5, turn. Sk 3 sc, 1 sc in last st (button lp made), fasten off.

Work 5 sc on top center of front pc strip for 2 rows, fasten off.

FINISHING
1. Cut a length of bead trim to fit the bag front. Hand-stitch the ribbon heading of the bead trim to the underside of a popcorn strip, so the beads hang below.
2. Align the bottom of the popcorn strip to the top of the bag front, so the beads dangle onto the right side of the front. Using a tapestry needle threaded with yarn, whipstitch the popcorn strip to the top of the bag front, stitching over the bead dangles.
3. Repeat steps 1 and 2 for the bag back.
4. Line the bag, if desired, following the directions on page 95.
5. Pin the gusset in place. Sewing from the right side, whipstitch the gusset to the back and front.
6. Sew the straps in place.
7. Sew on the button.

Silk Victorian Pouch

Lacy Victorian-style pouches make wonderful

evening bags. Crocheted from a luxurious silk

yarn, this lovely bag would be a great accent

to a little black dress.

YARN
Lightweight silk yarn

Shown: Silk Purse by Alchemy, 100% silk, 1.75 oz (50 g)/138 yd (127 m): Persimmon #005F, 1 skein

HOOK
3/D (3.25 mm)

STITCHES USED
Single crochet

Half double crochet

GAUGE
6 small shells = 4" (10 cm)

NOTIONS
Stitch markers

Tapestry needle

Glass beads

Shown: A Touch of Glass from CCA of America

FINISHED SIZE
5^1/$_2$" x 7^1/$_2$" (14 x 19.3 cm)

Silk yarn in half-double-crochet shell stitches.

BODY

Bag is worked in rnds, starting at bottom.

Foundation rnd: Ch 4, join with Sl st to form ring. Work 8 sc in ring, pm for beg of rnds, bring up marker at end of each rnd, do not join after each rnd.

Rnd 1: Sc, inc every st (16 sc).

Rnd 2: Sc, inc every other st (24 sc).

Rnd 3: Sc, inc every third st (32 sc).

Rnd 4: Sc, inc every fourth st (40 sc).

Cont working sc in rnds, inc 8 sts every rnd in this manner, always having 1 more st bet inc until you have 72 sts.

Work 1 rnd on 72 sts, through BL (this row denotes where shell st will be picked up later).

Cont working sc in rnds on 72 sts for 1" (2.5 cm) more. On last row, dec 4 sc, evenly spaced on row (68 sc), join with Sl st at end of last rnd.

Beg openwork shell patt as foll:

The rnd of hdc shells begins and ends with a half shell.

Drawstring woven through holes in shell stitch row.

Foundation row: Ch 2, 1 hdc same st as ch 2 (half of shell), * sk 3 sts, 2 hdc, ch 1, 2 hdc in next st (shell st made), rep from * around, end 2 hdc in same st as beg ch 2 (this completes shell), ch 1, join with Sl st to top of beg ch 2 (17 shells made).

Rnd 1: Ch 2, 1 hdc slightly behind ch 2 in ch-1 sp before joining (half of shell), * 2 hdc, ch 1, 2 hdc in next ch-1 sp, rep from * around, end 2 hdc in same ch-1 sp as beg, to complete shell.

Rep rnd 1 for 15 rnds more.

Work 1 more rnd of shell patt, making each shell 3 hdc, ch 2, 3 hdc, fasten off.

DRAWSTRINGS
Make two.
Using double strand of yarn, ch 80, fasten off.

FINISHING
1. Work a shell row of 3 hdc, ch 2, 3 hdc around the bottom in the front loop of the round previously worked through the back loop.
2. Make a tassel, following the directions on page 45. Stitch the tassel to the bottom center of the pouch.
3. Weave a drawstring through the holes in the fifth row from the top, tie the ends together and add beads to the tails. Repeat with the other drawstring, from the opposite side of the bag.

Blooming Granny Squares

The granny square has always been the best-loved

crochet motif. Here it's gone floral and is hooked

in brights popping against a black background. This

bag would also look great in pastels or naturals.

YARN
Lightweight cotton yarn

Shown: Cotton Classic by Tahki/Stacy Charles, 100% cotton, 1.75 oz (50 g)/108 yd (100 m): green #3760 (C), 2 skeins; black #3002 (D), 2 skeins. Use small amounts of several other colors (A, B) for centers of squares.

HOOK
5/F (3.75 mm)

STITCHES USED
Single crochet

Double crochet

Popcorn

GAUGE
1 square = 4" x 4" (10 x 10 cm)

NOTIONS
½ yd (0.5 m) lining (optional)

½ yd (0.5 m) fleece or felt (optional)

Sewing needle and thread (optional)

Tapestry needle

Oval ring handles, 3" x 5" (7.5 x 12.7 cm) opening

FINISHED SIZE
12" x 14" (30.5 x 35.5 cm)

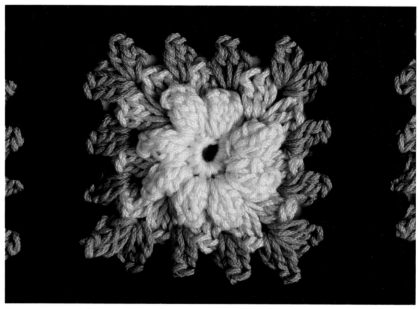

Granny square with flower-motif center.

GRANNY SQUARE
Make 18.

Rnds 4 and 5 will always be worked using C and D. Rnds 1, 2, 3, and foundation rnd will vary in color choices. Once center flower is completed, it is necessary to square off. This is accomplished by beg rnd with a half corner, working 3 corners around, and ending with another half corner. Rnds 3, 4, and 5 are worked in this manner.

Foundation rnd: With A, ch 4, join with Sl st to form ring. Work 8 sc in ring, join with Sl st.

Rnd 1 (pc rnd): Ch 3 (counts as a dc), 4 dc in same st as ch 3, complete as pc, ch 1 * pc in next st, ch 1, rep from * 6 times more (8 pc sts in rnd), join with Sl st to top of beg ch 3, fasten off A.

Rnd 2: Join B in any ch-1 sp, ch 3 (counts as a dc now and throughout), 2 more dc in same sp (half corner) * 3 dc in next ch-1 sp, 3 dc, ch 1, 3 dc in next ch-1 sp (corner), rep from * 2 times more, end 3 dc in next ch-1 sp, 3 dc in same sp as beg ch 1, join with Sl st to top of beg ch 3 (this completes last corner), fasten off B.

Rnd 3: Join C in any ch-1 sp, ch 3, 2 more dc in same sp (half corner), * 3 dc in next ch-1 sp, 3 dc in next ch-1 sp, 3 dc, ch 1, 3 dc in next ch-1 sp (corner), rep from * 2 times more, end 3 dc in next ch-1 sp, 3 dc in next ch-1 sp, 3 dc in same sp as beg ch 1, join with Sl st to top of beg ch 3, fasten off C.

Rnd 4: Join D in any ch-1 sp, ch 3, 2 more dc in same sp (half corner) * [3 dc in next ch-1 sp] 3 times, 3 dc, ch 1, 3 dc in next ch-1 sp (corner), rep from * 2 times more, end [3 dc in next ch-1 sp] 3 times, 3 dc in same sp as beg ch 1, join with Sl st to top of beg ch 3, fasten off D.

FRONT

Sew 9 squares together in 3 rows of 3 to form the bag front.

Using C, join yarn in top right corner, RS facing you, ch 3, work 14 dc in first square, 1 dc in seam, 15 dc in second square, 1 dc in seam, 15 dc in last square, ch 3, turn (47 dc).

Row 2: Sk first st, 1 dc dec in next 2 sts, dc in each st to last 3 sts, dc dec next 2, 1 dc in last st, ch 3, turn (45 dc).

Rows 3, 4, and 5: Rep row 2 (39 dc). Fasten off this color and join black. Cont to dec each side as established twice more (35 dc).

Work 2 rows even, fasten off, leaving a long end for sewing.

BACK

Work same as front.

GUSSET

Foundation row: Using C, ch 9. Starting in second ch from hook, work 1 sc in each ch to end (8 sc), ch 1, turn.

Row 1: Sk first st, sc in second st and in each st to end, 1 sc in top of tch (8 sc), ch 1, turn.

Rep row 1 until piece measures 36" (91.5 cm).

FINISHING

1. Line the bag, if desired, following the directions on page 95. Line only the rectangular area behind the granny squares, avoiding the upper section below the handles.

2. Pin the gusset between the front and back, stopping at the top of the squares. Sew the gusset in place.

3. Place a handle at the top of the front, and turn the last two rows of stitches to the inside over the handle. Stitch in place. Repeat for the other handle.

Shopper's Net Tote

European shoppers carry their purchases home in mesh

bags, and you can, too. Light but strong, this mesh tote is

made of a thrifty "kitchen cotton" yarn. It takes up little

room until you need it, then expands to hold a lot.

YARN

Medium weight cotton yarn

Shown: Sugar 'n Cream by Lily, 100% cotton, worsted weight, 2.5 oz (70 g)/120 yd (111 m): Dusty Rose #79, 4 skeins

HOOK

8/H (5 mm)

STITCH USED

Single crochet

GAUGE

3 openwork meshes = 4" (10 cm)

NOTIONS

Tapestry needle

FINISHED SIZE

16" x 18" (40.5 x 46 cm)

Medium weight cotton yarn in single crochet open-work mesh.

BACK AND FRONT

Join new yarn at row ends only, as yarn joined in center of work will not be easily concealed.

Foundation row: Ch 59 loosely. Starting in seventh ch from hook, make 1 sc, * ch 5, sk 3 ch, 1 sc in next ch, rep from * 12 times, end ch 5, sk 3, 1 sc in last ch, ch 7, turn.

Row 1: * Sc in third ch of ch 5, ch 5, rep from * 11 times, end 1 sc in fourth ch of beg ch 7, ch 7, turn.

Rep row 1 until piece is 36" (91.5 cm) long, fasten off.

DRAWSTRINGS

Cut three strands of yarn, each about 5 yd (4.6 m) long. Holding these strands together, fold in half and knot the ends together. Pin the knot to a padded, stationary surface. Holding the yarns at the fold, twist the yarns until they become tightly twisted and begin to crimp. Pinch the yarns at the center and bring the fold to the knot. Holding the twisted halves next to each other, release the center and allow the halves to twist together. Repeat to make a second drawstring.

FINISHING

1. Fold the bag body in half, wrong sides together, and sew side seams.

2. Weave one drawstring in and out of the open meshes in the fifth mesh row, beginning and ending on one side.

3. Knot the drawstring ends together a few inches from the end. Trim the ends and unwind to the knot, to form a tassel.

4. Repeat steps 2 and 3 for the other drawstring, starting from the opposite side of the bag, and going through the same holes.

Not Net
Tote Tagalong

This little bag is a great companion to your net shopping tote.

It gives you a place to carry your small essentials that would

fall through the holes in the net. This bag is also large enough

to store the folded-up net tote when it's not being used.

BACK

Foundation Row: Ch 36 loosely. Starting in second ch from hook, work 1 sc in each ch to end (35 sc), ch 1, turn.

Row 1: Sk first st (ch 1 counts as first st now and throughout), * 1 sc in next st, rep from * across, 1 sc in top of tch (35 sc), ch 1, turn.

Rep row 1 until piece is 6½" (16.3 cm) long, fasten off.

FRONT

Work same as back.

FINISHING

1. Sew Velcro to the wrong side of each piece, below the top row of stitches.

2. Holding back and front wrong sides together, working through both layers, work sc down one side, along the bottom, up the other side, do not fasten off. Continue working sc along the top edge on one side only. At end, ch 12 for loop, join Sl st at bottom of ch, cont along the other side of top edge, join with Sl st, fasten off.

Medium weight cotton yarn in single crochet.

YARN

Medium weight cotton yarn

Shown: Sugar 'n Cream by Lily, 100% cotton, 2.5 oz (70 g)/120 yd (111 m): Dusty Rose #79, 1 skein

HOOK

8/H (5 mm)

STITCH USED

Single crochet

GAUGE

13 sc = 4" (10 cm)

NOTIONS

12" (30.5 cm) Velcro for closure
Sewing needle and thread
Tapestry needle

FINISHED SIZE

10½" x 7" (26.7 x 18 cm)

Eight-Pocket Carryall

You can never have too many closets or too many

pockets. Get organized with this great big tote with

places for all your gadgets and essentials. Interesting

texture is created by alternating single and double

crochet stitches in one row, then working singles in the

doubles and doubles in the singles in the next row.

YARN

Medium weight cotton yarn

Shown: Lion Cotton, 100% cotton, 5 oz (140 g)/236 yd (212 m); Periwinkle #183 (MC), 4 skeins; Purple #147 (CC), 1 skein

HOOKS

9/I (5.5 mm)

8/H (5 mm)

STITCHES USED

Single crochet

Double crochet

GAUGE

13 sts = 4" (10 cm) on 9/I hook

NOTIONS

Tapestry needle

Button

FINISHED SIZE

16" x 12" x 3"
(40.5 x 30.5 x 7.5 cm)

Cotton yarn in alternating single and double crochet stiches.

BACK

Foundation row: With 9/I hook and MC, ch 53 loosely. Work 1 sc in third ch from hook, * 1 dc in next ch, 1 sc in next ch, rep from * end 1 sc in last ch, ch 3, turn (counts as a dc).

Row 1: * Work 1 sc in next dc, 1 dc in next sc, rep from * across, ending 1 sc in top of tch. Ch 3 (counts as dc), turn.

Rep row 1 for patt. Work patt for 11½" (29.3 cm), fasten off.

FRONT

Work same as back.

GUSSET

With 9/I hook and MC, ch 13. Work patt for 38" (96.5 cm), fasten off.

LARGE POCKETS

Make two.
With 9/I hook and MC, ch 53. Work patt for 6" (15 cm), fasten off.

SIDE POCKETS

Make two.
With 9/I hook and MC, ch 13. Work patt for 6½" (16.3 cm), fasten off.

STRAPS
Make two.
With 9/I hook and CC, ch 7. Work patt for 45" (115 cm), fasten off.

BUTTON TAB
With 9/I hook and MC, ch 13. Work patt for 3½" (9 cm).

Next row: Work patt for 3 sts, ch 4, sk 4, work patt for last 3 sts, ch 1, turn.

Next row: Work 1 sc in each of first 3 sts, 4 sc under ch-4 lp, sc in last 3 sts, fasten off.

FINISHING
1. Using 8/H hook and CC, work 1 row sc at the top edge of all the pockets.
2. Sew the front and back pockets in place.
3. Fold the gusset in half, pin at the center bottom, pin the sides in place. Working from right side, starting at the top edge, with 8/H hook and CC, working through both layers, work sc down one side, along the bottom, up the other side. Work the other side to correspond.
4. Sew the side pockets in place on the gusset.
5. Sew the straps in place, sewing through the pocket and bag to form divisions in the large pocket.
6. Using MC and 8/H hook, work 1 row sc around the entire top of the bag.
7. Sew the tab in place. Sew on the button.

Ninth Pocket

When eight pockets are not enough, this little buttoned-up

pouch is number nine. It is made with the same stitch pattern

as the Eight-Pocket Carryall.

BACK

Foundation Row: With 9/I hook, ch 25. Work 1 sc in third ch from hook, * 1 dc in next ch, 1 sc in next ch, rep from * 10 times, end 1 sc in last ch (22 sc), ch 3, turn (counts as dc).

Row 1: * Work 1 sc in next dc, 1 dc in next sc, rep from * across, ending 1 sc in top of tch. Ch 3 (counts as dc), turn.

Rep row 1 for 4" (10 cm), pm, cont for 2" (5 cm) more.

Next row: Sk first st, work patt on next 9 sts, ch 5, sk 2 sts (button loop), work patt on rem 10 sts, fasten off.

FRONT

Work same as back for 4" (10 cm), fasten off.

FINISHING

1. Place the bag front and back wrong sides together, with the upper edge of the front even with the marker on the back. Starting at the top right corner, working through both layers, sc down the side, across the bottom, and up the other side.

2. Fold the extra 2" (5 cm) toward the front for a flap. Sew on the button.

YARN

Medium cotton yarn

Shown: Lion Cotton, 100% cotton, 5 oz (140 g)/236 yd (212 m); Purple #147, 1 skein

HOOKS

9/I (5.5 mm)

8/H (5 mm)

STITCHES USED

Single crochet

Double crochet

GAUGE

13 sts = 4" (10 cm) on 9/I hook

NOTIONS

Stitch markers

Tapestry needle

Button

FINISHED SIZE

4½" x 6¾" (11.5 x 17 cm)

Crochet Stitches

SLIP KNOT AND CHAIN

All crochet begins with a chain, into which is worked the foundation row for your piece. To make a chain, start with a slip knot. To make a slip knot, make a loop several inches from the end of the yarn, insert the hook through the loop, and catch the tail with the end **(1)**. Draw the yarn through the loop on the hook **(2)**. After the slip knot, start your chain. Wrap the yarn over the hook (yarn over) and catch it with the hook. Draw the yarn through the loop on the hook. You have now made 1 chain.

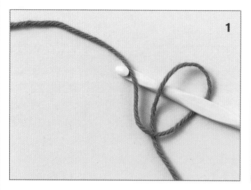

Repeat the process to make a row of chains. When counting chains, do not count the slip knot at the beginning or the loop that is on the hook **(3)**.

SLIP STITCH

The slip stitch is a very short stitch that is mainly used to join two pieces of crochet together when working in rounds. To make a slip stitch, insert the hook into the specified stitch, wrap the yarn over the hook **(1)**, and then draw the yarn through the stitch and the loop already on the hook **(2)**.

SINGLE CROCHET

Insert the hook into the specified stitch, wrap the yarn over the hook, and draw the yarn through the stitch so there are 2 loops on the hook **(1)**. Wrap the yarn over the hook again and draw the yarn through both loops **(2)**. When working in single crochet, always insert the hook through both top loops of the next stitch, unless the directions specify front loop or back loop only.

SINGLE CROCHET 2 STITCHES TOGETHER

This decreases the number of stitches in a row or round by 1. Insert the hook into the specified stitch, wrap the yarn over the hook, and draw the yarn through the stitch so there are 2 loops on the hook. Insert the hook through the next stitch, wrap the yarn over the hook, and draw the yarn through the stitch so there are 3 loops on the hook **(1)**. Wrap the yarn over the hook again and draw the yarn through all the loops at once **(2)**.

 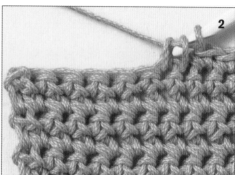

REVERSE SINGLE CROCHET

This stitch is usually used to create a border. At the end of a row, chain 1 but do not turn. Working backward, insert the hook into the previous stitch **(1)**, wrap the yarn over the hook, and draw the yarn through the stitch so there are 2 loops on the hook. Wrap the yarn over the hook again and draw the yarn through both loops. Continue working in the reverse direction **(2)**.

HALF DOUBLE CROCHET

Wrap the yarn over the hook, insert the hook into the specified stitch, and wrap the yarn over the hook again **(1)**. Draw the yarn through the stitch so there are 3 loops on the hook. Wrap the yarn over the hook and draw it through all 3 loops at once **(2)**.

DOUBLE CROCHET

Wrap the yarn over the hook, insert the hook into the specified stitch, and wrap the yarn over the hook again. Draw the yarn through the stitch so there are 3 loops on the hook **(1)**. Wrap the yarn over the hook again and draw it through 2 of the loops so there are now 2 loops on the hook **(2)**. Wrap the yarn over the hook again and draw it through the last loops **(3)**.

TRIPLE CROCHET

Wrap the yarn over the hook twice, insert the hook into the specified stitch, and wrap the yarn over the hook again. Draw the yarn through the stitch so there are 4 loops on the hook. Wrap the yarn over the hook again **(1)** and draw it through 2 of the loops so there are now 3 loops on the hook **(2)**. Wrap the yarn over the hook again and draw it through 2 of the loops so there are now 2 loops on the hook **(3)**. Wrap the yarn over the hook again and draw it through the last 2 loops **(4)**.

POPCORN STITCH 1

This version is worked from the right side.

Make 5 double crochets in the specified stitch, draw up the last loop slightly, and remove the hook **(1)**. Insert the hook into the first of the 5 double crochets made, pick up the dropped loop, and draw it through. Chain 1 **(2)**.

POPCORN STITCH 2

This version is worked from the wrong side. Wrap the yarn over the hook, pick up a loop in the next stitch, yarn over and through 2 loops. [Wrap the yarn over the hook, pick up a loop in the same stitch, yarn over and through 2 loops] 2 times. Wrap the yarn over the hook and draw it through all 4 loops on the hook **(1)**.

BULLION STITCH

Chain 3. Wrap the yarn loosely around the hook 10 times, insert the hook in the next stitch, yarn over and draw up a loop **(1)**. Wrap the yarn over the hook again and carefully draw through the coil of loops on the hook. You may find it necessary to pick the loops off the hook with your fingers, 1 at a time **(2)**. Yarn over the hook again and draw through the remaining stitch.

SHELL STITCH

Make 2 double crochets, chain 1, and then work 2 double crochets in the same stitch (shown).

FRONT POST DOUBLE CROCHET

This stitch follows a row of double crochet.

Chain 3 to turn. Wrap the yarn over the hook. Working from the front, insert the hook from right to left (left to right for left-handed crocheters) under the post of the first double crochet from the previous row, and pick up a loop (shown). Wrap the yarn over the hook and complete the stitch as a double crochet.

Left-handed.

Right-handed.

BACK POST DOUBLE CROCHET

This stitch follows a row of double crochet.

Chain 3 to turn. Wrap the yarn over the hook. Working from the back, insert the hook from right to left (left to right for left-handed crocheters) under the post of the first double crochet from the previous row, and pick up a loop (shown). Wrap the yarn over the hook and complete the stitch as a double crochet.

Left-handed.

Right-handed.

PICOT STITCH

Used as an edging.

* Chain 3, work 1 single crochet in the first chain **(1)**, skip 1 stitch, and work 1 single crochet in the next stitch. Repeat from * across the row **(2)**.

BASIC TUNISIAN STITCH

Each row has 2 halves: picking up the loops and working them off.

Make a chain of the desired length.

Row 1 (first half): Keeping all loops on the hook, skip the first chain from the hook (the loop on the hook is the first chain) and draw up a loop in each chain across **(1)**. Do not turn.

Row 1 (second half): Wrap the yarn over the hook and draw it through the first loop. * Wrap the yarn over the hook and draw it through the next 2 loops. Repeat from * across until 1 loop remains. The loop that remains on the hook always counts as the first stitch of the next row **(2)**.

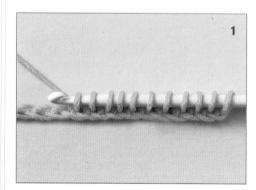
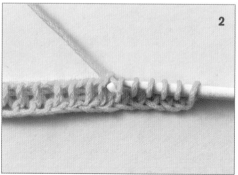

Row 2 (first half): Keeping all loops on the hook, skip the first vertical bar and draw up a loop under the next vertical bar and under each vertical bar across **(3)**.

Row 2 (second half): Work the same as the second half of row 1.

Repeat row 2 for basic Tunisian stitch.

TUNISIAN AND SHELLS

Chain the number of stitches directed in the pattern.

Row 1 (foundation half shells, wrong side): Work 4 double crochets in the fourth chain from the hook (makes a half shell at the beginning of the row), * skip 3 chains, work 1 single crochet in next chain, skip 3 chains, and work 9 double crochets in next chain (makes a half shell). Repeat from * until 8 chains remain. Skip 3 chains, work 1 single crochet in the next chain, skip 3 chains, and work 5 double crochets in last chain (makes a half shell at the end of the row). Chain 1 and turn **(1)**.

Row 2 (Tunisian stitch, right side): * [Draw up a loop in the next stitch and retain the loop on the hook] 5 times (6 loops on the hook), draw up a loop in the next stitch and draw this loop through the first loop on the hook, forming an upright stitch or bar. [Yarn over and through 2 loops] 5 times *. There will be 6 bars in the row, and 1 loop left on the hook. The loop on the hook and the bar below it count as the first stitch. ** Retaining the loops on the hook, draw up a loop in each of the next 5 bars (6 loops on the hook), draw up a loop in the next stitch, and draw this loop through the first loop on the hook. [Yarn over and through 2 loops] 5 times. Repeat from ** 2 times. There will be 4 rows of bars **(2)**. Insert the hook in the second bar, yarn over and through the bar and the loop on the hook (1 stitch bound off), bind off 4 more stitches, and work 1 single crochet in the next stitch. Repeat from *, ending with a single crochet in the top of the turning chain. Chain 1 and turn. You now have blocks of Tunisian crochet between half shells **(3)**.

Row 3: Skip the first stitch (chain 1 counts as the first stitch), work 1 single crochet in each stitch across the row, and work 1 single crochet in turning chain. Chain 3 and turn **(4)**.

continued

Row 4 : Yarn over, draw up a loop in the second single crochet, yarn over and through 2 loops on the hook, [yarn over and draw up a loop in the next stitch, yarn over and through 2 loops] 3 times, yarn over and through 5 loops on the hook, and chain 1 tightly for the eye of the half shell **(5)**. * Chain 3, single crochet in the next stitch, chain 3, [yarn over and draw up a loop in the next stitch, yarn over and through 2 loops] 9 times, yarn over and through 10 loops on the hook, and chain 1 tightly to form the eye of the full shell. Repeat from * until all full shells are made. Chain 3, single crochet in the next stitch, chain 3, [yarn over and draw up a loop in the next stitch, yarn over and through 2 loops] 4 times, yarn over and through 5 loops, and chain 1 tightly to form the eye of the last half shell. Ch 3 and turn. You now have full shells between the Tunisian blocks **(6)**.

Row 5: Work 4 double crochets in the eye of the first half shell, skip chain 3, work 1 single crochet in the first single crochet, skip chain 3, * work 9 double crochets in the eye of the next shell, skip chain 3, work 1 single crochet in the next single crochet, and skip chain 3. Repeat from * until all the full shells are complete **(7)**. Skip chain 3, work 5 double crochets in the eye of last half shell, chain 1, and turn.

Repeat rows 2 through 5 for pattern.

LINING A CROCHETED BAG

Before you stitch the pieces of your bag together, it's a good idea to add lining. Besides keeping tiny things like coins and earrings from falling through the crochet stitches, lining also gives your bag extra body and helps it keep its shape. I use an interlining of fleece or felt to cushion and support the inside, and then I cover it with a silky lining.

1. Trace the outer edges of the main-bag pieces onto paper. Use this as a pattern to cut an interlining and a lining for each piece. Trim 1/2" (1.3 cm) from the edges of the interlining.

2. Center the interlining over the wrong side of the bag piece. Thread a sewing needle with all-purpose thread in a color to match the bag. Catch the interlining in place with a few stitches around the outer edge.

3. Center the lining, right side up, over the interlining. Turn under the edge all around so that it just covers the interlining. Pin the lining in place.

4. Stitch the lining to the bag, enclosing the interlining.

5. Complete steps 1 through 4 for each bag piece. Then finish the bag, following the project instructions.

Abbreviations

approx	approximately	**p**	picot
beg	begin/beginning	**patt**	pattern
bet	between	**pc**	popcorn
BL	back loop(s)	**pm**	place marker
BP	back post	**prev**	previous
BPdc	back post double crochet	**rem**	remaining
CC	contrasting color	**rep**	repeat
ch	chain	**rnd(s)**	round(s)
ch-	refers to chain or space previously made, e.g., ch-1 space	**RS**	right side(s)
		sc	single crochet
ch-sp	chain space	**sc 2tog**	single crochet 2 stitches together
CL	cluster		
cm	centimeter(s)	**sk**	skip
dc	double crochet	**Sl st**	slip stitch
dc 2tog	double crochet 2 stitches together	**sp(s)**	space(s)
		st(s)	stitch(es)
dec	decrease	**tch**	turning chain
FL	front loop(s)	**tbl**	through back loop
foll	follow/follows/following	**tog**	together
FP	front post	**tr**	treble crochet
FPdc	front post double crochet	**WS**	wrong side(s)
g	gram	**yd**	yard(s)
hdc	half double crochet	**yo**	yarn over
inc	increase/increases/increasing	**[ ]**	Work instructions within brackets as many times as directed
lp(s)	loop(s)	**( )**	At end of row, indicates total number of stitches worked
m	meter(s)		
MC	main color	*****	Repeat instructions following the single asterisk as directed
mm	millimeter(s)		
oz	ounce(s)	******	Repeat instructions between asterisks as many times as directed or repeat from a given set of instructions